Where is the Tower of London?

by Janet B. Pascal

illustrated by David Malan

Penguin Workshop
An Imprint of Penguin Random House

For Erica, and about time, too!—JBP

For Penny, Emmett, Calvin, and Alice—DM

PENGUIN WORKSHOP
Penguin Young Readers Group
An Imprint of Penguin Random House LLC

Library of Congress Cataloging-in-Publication Data is available.

ISBN 9781524786069 (paperback)   10 9 8 7 6 5 4 3 2 1
ISBN 9781524786083 (library binding)   10 9 8 7 6 5 4 3 2 1

Contents

Where Is the Tower of London?

In 1934, a song called "With Her Head Tucked Underneath Her Arm" became popular in England. The song was about a ghostly woman. Every night she could be seen gliding along the halls of the Bloody Tower in London. Her head had been chopped off, and she carried it under her arm like a soccer ball.

Who was the song talking about? A queen. A queen of England. Her name was Anne Boleyn. She was one of the wives of King Henry VIII, who had her head cut off in 1536. The Bloody Tower is part of the great Tower of London. It earned its name even before the days of Anne Boleyn. Two children who were imprisoned there were murdered. Many others suffered the same fate as those children and Anne Boleyn. Others were hanged or tortured.

Anne Boleyn and King Henry VIII

1

But the Tower of London is not just a prison where many people met bloody deaths. It has also been a grand palace, an armory for weapons, a jewel storehouse, and a zoo. It has stood for almost a thousand years. During

this time, it has been the home of kings and princes. For years, all the coins in England were made here. It has the world's most famous diamond on display. And the first elephant in England lived here.

CHAPTER 1
William the Conqueror

The one date that every English schoolchild knows is 1066. This is the year William the Conqueror became king of England. It marks the beginning of modern English history.

William the Conqueror

Before 1066, people in England were known as Anglo-Saxons. One of their last kings was named Edward the Confessor. (All Anglo-Saxon kings had names like this. Edward's father was called Ethelred the Unready because he always lost battles against invaders.)

Edward was a very good man. He ruled for many years. After his death, he was made a saint. Unfortunately, he did not have any children to leave his throne to. And he did not give clear instructions about who should rule after him. A powerful Anglo-Saxon lord named Harold Godwinson took the throne after Edward died.

Harold Godwinson's coronation

However, over in Normandy, part of northern France, another lord believed *he* should be England's next king. This was William, the Duke of Normandy. (He later became known as William the Conqueror.) William was only Edward's second cousin, once removed. So he was not a close relative. He was not next in line for the throne. But William swore Edward had promised the throne to him.

William and the Normans invaded England, landing on the southern shore. In the Battle of

Hastings, they defeated the Anglo-Saxon army. Harold was killed. William was now king of England. He took large areas of land that had belonged to Anglo-Saxon lords and gave them to his followers. Of course, the Anglo-Saxon lords were very angry about this. Many of them were ready to fight William to take back their country. They wanted an Anglo-Saxon king. William knew he could only hold on to England if he and his men were strong, protected themselves from their enemies, and were always prepared to fight.

So William started building fortresses all over England. People think there may have been as many as five hundred of them. These forts would keep him safe from the angry, conquered people. And soldiers living in the forts would quickly stop any people who tried to protest.

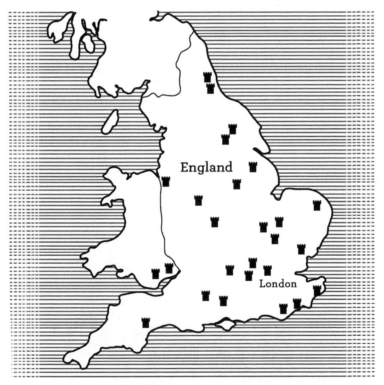

Important forts built by William the Conqueror

William was crowned in London, the city where England's kings lived. During the ceremony, a hostile crowd of London citizens protested outside. A group of William's men with swords had to rush out to stop them. This showed William that he needed to build his strongest fort in London, to control its citizens and keep him safe from angry mobs.

CHAPTER 2
Building the Tower

The spot William chose for his fort had already been built on almost a thousand years before he was born. London was settled by the ancient Romans around the time that they conquered England, in the year AD 43. It was a good place for a city. It was on flat ground that was easy to defend, and it was right on the river Thames, so it was easy for ships to reach. It soon became the biggest and the richest city in England.

In the second century, the Romans built a great wall around their city to protect it. By the time William the Conqueror arrived, the Romans had left England hundreds of years before. But some of their London wall was still there. When William built his fort in London, he used the

Roman wall as part of it. It is still there today. This means that the oldest parts of the Tower of London are almost two thousand years old.

William's original building was probably what is called a *motte and bailey* castle. A motte is a hill. If there wasn't a natural hill where the Normans wanted a castle, they would pile up earth to create one. On the top of the hill, they built a fortress. All around the hill, they dug a deep ditch. The area inside the ditch was called the bailey. Around the whole thing, they built a wooden fence.

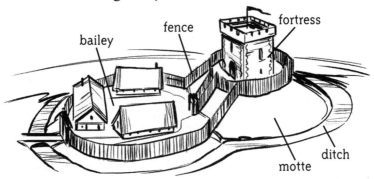

The original tower that William built in London was finished in only three days. It was made of wood. Soon William decided that he needed something stronger to impress the people of the city. In place of the wooden tower, he decided to build a great stone tower.

He chose a monk named Gundulf to design it. The tower Gundulf built was called the White Tower. He used pale white stone imported all the way from Normandy. It was the biggest building in all of England that wasn't a church. It could be seen from miles away. It was ninety feet tall with a smaller tower at each corner. The walls of the building were fifteen feet thick at the bottom.

The most important thing about the Tower was that it was a strong fort. To keep everyone safe, there was only one entrance. This was a wooden staircase leading to the middle floor, where a group of soldiers lived. The staircase could be pulled up if necessary. Then no one could get in. The bottom floor stored arms and armor.

The Tower was also a grand castle where the king and his family could live. The upper floor was made rich and comfortable for them. The whole tower was put in the charge of a man called the Constable of the Tower.

King Edward I's bedchamber

Over the years, many smaller towers and buildings grew up around the first tower. In 1097, King William II added a wall that ran all around the outer edge. In the 1220s and 30s, Henry III added ten new towers and a special ditch called a moat. It was filled with water and surrounded the wall. He also had the White Tower painted with whitewash in 1241, so it was truly gleaming white.

Starting in 1275, Edward I added a second wall closing in a large area around the first wall. This meant the Tower was surrounded by two rings of walls. Attackers would have to break through both of them before they could reach the White Tower.

When these kings were finished, in 1285, the Tower of London looked more or less the way it still does today. Gundulf's huge White Tower stood in the center. It gave the whole collection of buildings and walls its name: the Tower of London.

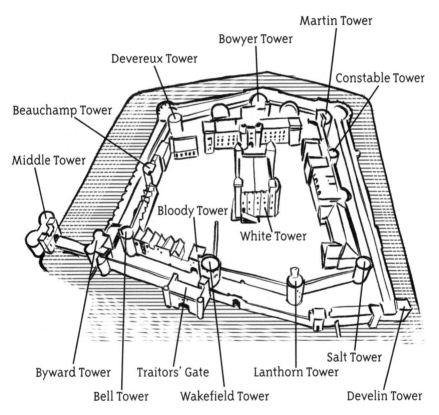

Martin Tower

Bowyer Tower

Devereux Tower

Constable Tower

Beauchamp Tower

Middle Tower

Bloody Tower

White Tower

Byward Tower

Traitors' Gate

Lanthorn Tower

Salt Tower

Bell Tower

Wakefield Tower

Develin Tower

How to Go to the Bathroom in a Castle

The White Tower has the oldest surviving garderobe in England. A garderobe was the place in a castle where people went to the bathroom. Castles had very thick walls. A hole in the wall ran from the garderobe down through the wall and out to the moat or to a specially dug pit. On any floor in the castle, you could sit on a seat cut into the wall, and the waste would drop all the way down.

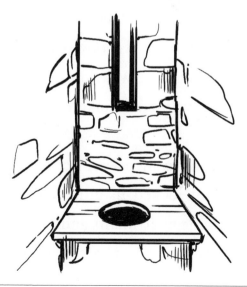

CHAPTER 3
Prisoners and Rebels

The Tower was built to defend the king and for his family to live in. But it soon took on a third role. It became a place to keep prisoners. It was not an ordinary jail. You wouldn't find common crooks like thieves or murderers there. It was the place where the king put political prisoners. These were people who the king thought threatened his power. They might disagree with what he was doing. Or he might be afraid they wanted to take the throne away from him.

Many of the prisoners were rich and powerful. They were not locked in dungeon cells. They had comfortable apartments and servants. They could walk around the gardens. One prisoner

even planted his own herb garden.

The first prisoner we know of was a man named Ranulf Flambard. He lived when William the Conqueror's son, William Rufus, was king. William Rufus was cruel and greedy. He took as much money in taxes from his people as he possibly could. Flambard was one of the main tax collectors. Most of Flambard's time was spent squeezing money out of the king's subjects. Everyone hated him.

One day while hunting, King William Rufus was killed by an arrow shot by one of his own men. People claimed it was just an accident.

Now William Rufus's younger brother took the throne. His name was Henry. Henry wanted the people of England to support him. So he arrested Flambard and locked him in the Tower. This arrest helped win support for Henry.

After Flambard had been in prison for six months, he came up with a plan to escape. He had a rope smuggled to him in a barrel of oysters. He gave a party for his guards and got them very drunk. Then he used the rope to climb out the window. He had arranged for a horse to be waiting for him. He rode away to freedom. So the first important prisoner in the Tower was also the first one to escape.

Some prisoners were kings of other countries. When a king was captured, his country was supposed to ransom him. This means they paid the English government a lot of money to have their king set free.

Even while they were captives, the kings continued to live like kings. For example, in 1357 a French king, John the Good, was a prisoner in the Tower. On his first day there, he and his followers were fed with seventy-four loaves of bread, twenty-one gallons of wine, three sheep, one calf, and thirteen chickens.

Writers in the Tower

Some of the people held in the Tower used the time they were locked up to write books. Sir Walter Raleigh is the most famous of these. He wrote several long poems and his *History of the World* while in the Tower. Other people just wrote on the walls. In the Tower today, you can still see the names, drawings, and comments carved into the stone by prisoners.

Sir Walter Raleigh

CHAPTER 4
Besieged!

Sometimes the Tower had to protect the king from his own subjects. For most of his reign, King Henry III was fighting a war against the powerful lords who owned land in England. In 1267, a group of lords surrounded the Tower of London. Using catapults, they tried to break through the thick walls. But they were beaten back.

King Henry III

Many of the fighters who helped the king win this battle were Jewish. The church didn't allow Christians to lend money for interest. So only Jewish people

Soldiers firing stones from a catapult at the Tower

could lend money. The kings of England often needed to borrow money. So they let Jewish moneylenders live in the area around the Tower.

Over the years, a large Jewish community grew up there. They were under the protection of the Constable of the Tower. When they were threatened, the Jews would go into the Tower, where they would be safe. So when the rebel lords' army attacked, these Jews fled to the Tower. There they bravely helped with the defense.

In 1290, King Edward I kicked all the Jews out of England. But the road near the Tower where they lived is still called Old Jewry.

Old Jewry Road, present day

In 1380, the government needed extra money because of the cost of fighting a long war known as the Hundred Years' War. So the new king, Richard II, declared a new tax. Everyone over fifteen years old in the kingdom had to pay one shilling. This was not much for a rich man. But for a poor worker, it was a full month's wages.

The peasants were already poor and starving. They had had enough. Headed by a leader named Wat Tyler, an army of more than twenty thousand peasants marched on London. Another army

of almost seventy thousand, led by Jack Straw, marched on London from another direction.

King Richard II was only fourteen years old. He went into the Tower to be safe. The peasant army raged through London. They burned and destroyed the palaces of government officials. They killed anyone who looked rich or powerful. But the Tower of London was too strong for them. They couldn't break in.

King Richard said he would meet with the peasant army outside London.

He bravely rode out of the Tower on his horse to the meeting place they had agreed on. But when the guards tried to close the Tower gates after the king had left, four hundred peasants were able to storm in. For the first time in its history, the Tower of London had an enemy army inside its walls.

In the Tower, the peasants found four of the government officials they hated most. They were hiding in the chapel. The peasants dragged them

outside and cut their heads off on Tower Hill. These were the first executions to take place at the Tower of London. They would not be the last.

Meanwhile, Richard was talking peacefully with the peasant army. He promised he would give them anything reasonable that they asked for. But on the way back, he heard about what had happened in the Tower. Now he was angry. He arranged to meet with the peasant leaders again. This time, fighting broke out and Wat Tyler was killed.

With their leader dead, the peasant army was ready to return home. They thought that Richard would keep his promise to them. But Richard said his promise didn't count because he had been forced to make it. He didn't keep it. The Peasants' Revolt didn't really change anything.

Years later, in 1399, Richard II returned to the Tower for a very different reason. When he grew up, he was a weak and flawed king. The throne was taken away from him by Henry IV. Henry put Richard in prison in the Tower. While Richard was locked up, Henry forced him to agree to give up his claim to be king.

Henry IV

Order of the Bath

For his coronation in 1399, Henry IV created a special honor, called the Knights of the Bath. The name meant exactly what it said. The night before the ceremony, forty-six tubs of water were laid out in the Tower. The forty-six men being honored each had to take a bath to purify himself. Then they were given their new title.

CHAPTER 5
The Menagerie

When people think of the Tower of London, they usually think about human prisoners. But not only people were locked in the Tower.

For hundreds of years, the king's private zoo—called the Menagerie—was located in the Tower. The first animals were lions that arrived around the year 1210. People thought that lions were very noble animals. The lion was on the royal

crest of England. So lions were a good choice for the king to own. In 1235, the European emperor Frederick II gave King Henry III three leopards as a present. Henry put them in the Tower. Then he decided to add some other animals. Soon he also had lynxes, lions, and camels.

The king of Norway gave Henry a big bear that was pure white. No one in England had seen a polar bear before. Finding enough fish for the

bear was hard. The keepers decided to let it catch its own food. Some of the gates in the Tower were water gates that opened right onto the river Thames. The keepers chained the bear to a water gate. Soon the people of London were treated to the amazing sight of a polar bear fishing for salmon in the Thames.

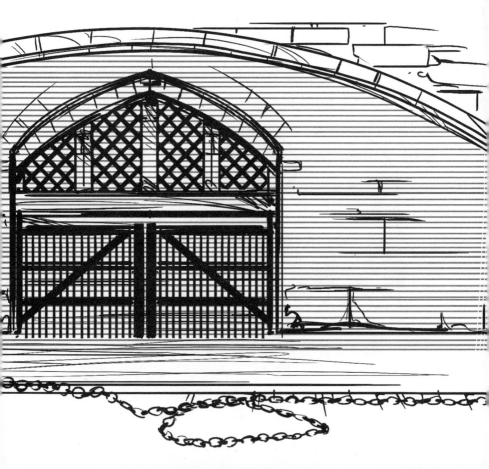

The French king Louis IX gave Henry an animal like nothing people had ever seen—one that ate and drank using its long trunk. This was the first elephant in England. It was not easy to ship such a large animal to London. After sailing on a boat to England, the elephant had to walk many miles to London. Huge crowds gathered to watch it go by. Unfortunately, no one really knew how to take care of an elephant. Hoping to keep it healthy, its keepers had it drink a gallon of wine a day. It only lived for two years.

Soon the king had so many animals that he decided he needed to build them a real home. One of the towers was turned into a zoo. It was called the Lion Tower. For many years, the gate in the Lion Tower was the only way people could get into the Tower. So anyone going to see the king had to pass by cages of lions and tigers.

The animals weren't treated the way we treat zoo animals today. They lived in bare cages. Sometimes they were let out to fight with each other. Or a lion would be put into a cage with some dogs, to see which was stronger. But the animals didn't always cooperate. One time a lamb was put in with a lion. The lion just sniffed it and then lay down and ignored it.

Of all the animals, the lions were treated with the greatest care. People believed that when a lion died, it meant the king or queen would soon die. So the keepers tried very hard to keep the lions healthy.

The zoo in the Tower lasted for about six hundred years. It grew until it contained many animals. These included a porcupine and a kangaroo. It became a big attraction. At first only people the king invited could see the zoo. Later on, any tourist could pay to see the animals. People think that the famous writer William Shakespeare might have visited the zoo. In his play *Hamlet* he describes a porcupine. The Tower was one of the only places in England where he could have seen one.

In the 1700s, a room was built where people and monkeys could mix together. The monkeys were running loose. This lasted until a monkey attacked a small boy. Sometimes the animals fought each other. A rare bird had its head bitten off when it leaned into the cage of a hyena. People got hurt, too. A girl was killed when she tried to pat a lion's paws. A small child was chased by a wolf that escaped from its cage.

Then the Duke of Wellington was put in charge of the Tower. He was a famous soldier. He thought it was silly to keep all those animals in a place that was supposed to be a military site. So he had the animals sent

Duke of Wellington

away to the London Zoo. By 1835, the Tower zoo was gone.

Ravens

One creature that lives in the Tower is especially important. This is a big black bird, similar to a crow, called a raven. In early years, flocks of wild ravens lived in the Tower. It was believed to be very unlucky to kill a raven.

During the seventeenth century, the royal observatory was in the Tower. This was a place with special instruments for studying the heavens. The astronomers complained that the birds' droppings were bad for their telescope. But the king wasn't willing to get rid of the birds. So he built a new observatory in nearby Greenwich, instead. The astronomers moved, and the ravens stayed where they were.

Royal Greenwich Observatory

Legend says that as long as there are ravens living in the Tower, England will survive. Today seven pet ravens are kept in the Tower. Their wings are clipped so they can't fly away.

CHAPTER 6
The Two Little Princes in the Tower

Some people think that the ravens liked to live in the Tower because so many people were killed there. Dead bodies are food for ravens.

Two kinds of executions used to take place in the Tower. Ordinary people were hanged on the gallows. Lords and ladies had their heads cut off. Usually people were killed outside the walls, on Tower Hill, so that the crowds could watch. People thought of it as entertainment.

Very important people were allowed to be beheaded privately inside the Tower walls. It was a quick and relatively painless death, compared to other forms of execution. The victim paid the headsman beforehand. This was to be sure he did a good job. Sometimes he did a bad job, or the

ax wasn't sharp enough. Then it might take many strokes before the person's head was cut all the way off. After someone was beheaded, the executioner would hold the head up high, so everyone could see the person was dead.

There were not really all that many executions at the Tower. In its entire history, only about 135 people were put to death there. And only about nineteen of them were killed inside the Tower's walls. The rest were killed on Tower Hill, outside. But there were other ways to die in the Tower without being executed. Inside the Tower walls it was easy to get rid of an enemy secretly. Then the public could be told that the person had gotten sick and died. Or the death could be kept secret altogether.

One person who was secretly killed in the Tower was George Plantagenet, the duke of Clarence. He was convicted of treason against his brother, King Edward IV. This means the king

George Plantagenet

was afraid George was trying to take the throne away from him. George died in 1478 while he was being held in the Tower. The legend is that he was drowned in a barrel of wine. After his death, his daughter always wore a charm shaped like a barrel in his honor.

By far, the most famous people to be killed in secret in the Tower are the "two little princes." They were innocent children who got trapped in a struggle among powerful groups of men.

In 1483, King Edward IV died. He left behind two sons. The older child became King Edward V. But Edward was only twelve years old, not old enough to rule. A person called the regent ruled for him. Since the regent controlled the boy king, he was the one really ruling the country.

Edward's uncle Richard served as regent and also guardian of the young king. Richard, however, wanted to be king himself. So he had

Edward and Edward's nine-year-old brother (also named Richard) moved to the Tower. He said he put them there to keep them safe. But really the two boys were prisoners. For a while they were seen playing in the garden. Then they disappeared. Exactly what happened to them is a mystery.

Most people think they were murdered in the Tower. According to legend, they were smothered with pillows while they slept. The most likely murderer was their uncle, who went on to become King Richard III.

Richard III

Richard had a strong motive for murdering his nephew Edward. As long as Edward was alive, people could use the boy as an excuse to fight. They could try to get rid of Richard and put Edward back on the throne.

But some people think Richard wasn't the killer. They say the next king, Henry VII, was the real murderer. His claim to the throne was even more shadowy than Richard's. So Edward

Henry VII

was even more of a threat to him. But no one knows.

There were even stories that the little princes hadn't been killed at all. Two young men showed up several years later claiming to be the princes from the Tower. Some people believed them.

In 1674, workmen at the Tower dug up a box that held small skeletons. Most people believe these are the bones of the two little princes. If so, they were definitely murdered soon after they moved to the Tower.

But we will never know for sure who did it.

The tower where the boys were kept was

called the Garden Tower because it had its own garden. But after their deaths, it was renamed the Bloody Tower. And that's what it's been known as ever since.

CHAPTER 7
Gunpowder and Fire

The Tower of London has been the center for several government departments. In the Middle Ages, one of these was called the Privy Wardrobe. It started as the office in charge of the king's private possessions. This meant clothing and furniture. It also included treasure, documents, and arms and armor.

The importance of the Wardrobe grew and changed. It became the department that stored and kept track of all the weapons, armor, and gunpowder that the king would need if he went to war.

Some of the armor was so beautiful that it was put on display for people to admire. In the seventeenth century, an exhibit was set up. It

showed life-size figures of every ruler since William the Conqueror. They were all on horseback, and—except for Queen Elizabeth I— they were all dressed in their finest armor.

In 1666, a terrible fire broke out in London. It looked like the fire might reach the Tower. The Tower was full of half a million pounds of gunpowder. If all that gunpowder exploded at once, it would destroy the building. And it would take most of London with it.

Men from the navy quickly

began carrying gunpowder from the Tower to ships on the river Thames. From there, it could be floated to safety. This was a very dangerous job. The air was full of ashes and sparks. If a single one hit a barrel of gunpowder, the barrel would catch fire and explode. Then the whole area would go up in flames. Against the odds, the men safely got all the gunpowder away. And the fire was stopped before it reached the Tower.

Like most governments, the kings of England produced a lot of paperwork. For many years, all important papers were kept with the king, no matter where he was. The king didn't just live in one palace. He would move around the country, staying in various mansions along the way. And all these papers had to come with him wherever he went.

By the late thirteenth century, there were so many papers that this was impossible. So the papers were stored in the Tower. There was no special room for them, and no organized system to keep track of them. The papers had to compete for space with the gunpowder and the prisoners. They were just kept on the floor, all mixed up. It wasn't until the early twentieth century that the papers got their own building to be stored in.

CHAPTER 8
Making Money

The Tower also served as the mint—the place where the country's money was made. It was sensible to put the mint in the Tower of London. Coins were made of gold and silver. It was a good idea to keep all that precious metal in a very safe place while it was waiting to be made into coins.

Making coins was hard work. First the metal was melted and made into round, flat discs. Then a man put the blank disc on top of a die. This was a kind of mold with a picture carved on it. He put another carved die on top of the blank disc. Then another man hit the stack with a hammer, hard enough to drive an impression of the pictures into the metal.

It was important to be sure that all the coins were made with exactly the right amount of gold or silver. So every year, there was a trial. It was just like any other trial, with a courtroom and a judge. But the defendant that was being tried was the coins, not a person. The case was decided by a jury made up of experts in metal, who tested the coins' weight. This trial still goes on today.

King Henry VIII spent a lot of money, so he needed more coins to be made. He decided to make coins out of copper, coated with silver or gold. The coins would still be worth the same amount that they had been before. But it would take less precious metal to make them, so the king could make more coins from the same amount of silver or gold. All the coins had Henry's picture stamped on them. After they were in use for a while, the precious metal rubbed off and showed the copper underneath. So people gave Henry the nickname "Old Copper Nose."

English coins were very thin, and the edges weren't perfectly even. People used to clip tiny bits of silver off the edges and save them up. When they had enough silver, they would melt it down to create a fake new coin. Clipping coins was a serious crime.

In the 1660s, the mint started to use machines to make the coins. This was faster and easier. It also meant the edges of the coins were more even. The thin edges could be covered with a pattern of little grooves. That way no one could clip the edges off without it being noticed. Special edge-making machines were used. Everyone who worked in the mint had to swear not to tell anyone how these machines worked. That way, no one could make fake coins.

The king had all the
old coins in the country
returned to the mint
and remade into new
ones. This complicated
work was overseen by
Sir Isaac Newton.
Newton is famous
as one of the
greatest scientists
who ever lived. But

Sir Isaac Newton

for many years he was also the head of the mint.

The mint stayed at the Tower until 1810.
Then it needed more space, so it was moved to
Tower Hill, just outside the Tower.

CHAPTER 9
Crown Jewels

Gold and silver coins weren't the only valuable things stored at the Tower. The Crown Jewels were also kept there. The Crown Jewels were used during the ceremony when a ruler was crowned. They included the crown itself, scepters and orbs that the king or queen would hold, and many other objects. Everything was made of gold and silver, and thickly covered with precious stones. So the Crown Jewels were not only very beautiful, they were very, very valuable.

For many years, the Crown Jewels were kept in Westminster Abbey, the church where English rulers were crowned. They belonged to England's rulers, but only while they were reigning. They couldn't sell them, and they weren't allowed to take them out of Westminster Abbey. Only the jewels that the ruler owned personally were kept in the Tower.

Westminster Abbey

In the 1600s, England had a revolution. The king was overthrown, and for several years the country was ruled by Puritans. These were the same group of strict Protestants that would help settle North America. The Puritans didn't believe in kings, or in fancy, expensive decorations. In 1649, they cut off the head of King Charles I. Then they had all the Crown Jewels broken up. The metal was melted and made into coins. Almost the only thing from the Crown Jewels that survives from before the English Civil War is one silver spoon, used for pouring sacred oil.

In 1660, King Charles II was restored to the throne. He had to have all new Crown Jewels made so he could be crowned. From then on, the Crown Jewels were kept in the Tower, where they would be safe . . . or so people thought.

In 1671, a man named Thomas Blood almost managed to steal the Crown Jewels. He made friends with the keeper of the jewels and got himself invited to dinner. He asked if he could see the jewels. Then he hit the keeper with a wooden mallet and knocked him out. He put some of the Crown Jewels in a bag, and even stuffed one piece down his pants. Fortunately, he was captured on

his way out of the Tower, and put in prison. Later, when Thomas was taken before King Charles II, the king was so amused by his boldness and cleverness that he didn't punish him. He even gave him his own estate in Ireland.

The Crown Jewels can be seen in the Tower today. They are on display in a special building. The largest clear-cut diamond in the world, the Cullinan I, is set into the scepter. It can also be removed and worn separately. The diamond is almost two and a half inches long—about the

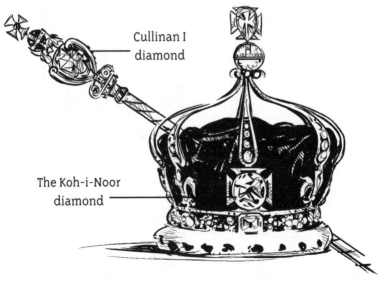

Cullinan I
diamond

The Koh-i-Noor
diamond

size of a chicken's egg—and worth about $400 million. The Koh-i-Noor, one of the world's most famous diamonds, is also in the collection, set into a crown. The Koh-i-Noor has a long history of being owned by various rulers. One legend says that whoever owns this diamond will rule the world. But only a woman can wear the diamond. It is bad luck for a man.

Queen Elizabeth II's Coronation

The last time the full set of Crown Jewels was used was in 1953, when Elizabeth II was crowned Queen of England. She had the crown changed a little to fit her better. The head size was made smaller, and the arches on the crown were lowered. She thought this made it look more feminine. In between coronations, the crown is used once every year. The queen wears it when she opens Parliament, the group that governs England.

CHAPTER 10
The Tudors

For more than a hundred years, starting in 1485, the rulers of England came from a family called the Tudors. It is because of the Tudors that most people today think of the Tower of London as a place of murder, torture, and execution. The Tudors didn't live in the Tower. It was no longer in good enough

Henry VIII

shape to serve as the main royal palace. But they sent many prisoners there. Henry VIII, in particular, had more people killed there than any other king. He ruled from 1509 to 1547.

Of all Henry's victims, the most famous are two of his wives. He had six wives altogether. English schoolchildren used to learn this little rhyme: "Divorced, beheaded, died. Divorced, beheaded, survived," to remember what happened to the various wives of Henry VIII.

His first wife was Catherine of Aragon. He was unhappy because she had only one child

who lived through infancy, and it was a girl. He wanted a son to be king after him. Then he fell in love with a lady-in-waiting named Anne Boleyn. He wanted to divorce Catherine and marry Anne. But the Catholic church did not allow divorce. The pope would not let him end his marriage.

So Henry said that the pope was no longer the head of the church in England. Henry was.

From then on, the church in England has been Anglican, not Catholic. And all because Henry wanted to marry Anne Boleyn.

As he prepared for his wedding, Henry had the Tower fixed up in Anne's honor. He added the four onion-shaped domes of the White Tower that are still there today.

Unfortunately, Anne didn't have a son, either, only a daughter. And Henry found that Anne was hot-tempered and independent. So he fell in love with another lady-in-waiting, Jane Seymour. Now

Jane Seymour

Henry wanted to get rid of Anne so he could marry Jane. He accused Anne of being a witch. He also said she had been unfaithful to him. He had one of the men he suspected thrown into the Tower and tortured. The prisoner was forced to say that he and Anne had a romantic relationship. He was also forced to accuse several other men. Anne and the men were all locked up in the Tower and sentenced to death.

Usually executions took place on Tower Hill. Crowds of people would gather to watch. But as a special favor to his wife, Henry decided that her execution would be private, inside the Tower walls. Before the execution, Anne was told that she would feel little pain. She answered, "I have heard that the executioner is very good. And I have a little neck."

Anne was praying as her head was struck off. When the executioner held the head up to show it to the people watching, it was said that her lips could still be seen moving in prayer.

Ten days after Anne died, Henry married Jane. Jane gave him the son and heir he wanted, but she died soon after giving birth. Henry's next wife was

Anne of Cleves

a foreign princess, Anne of Cleves. He had only seen a painting of her before their marriage. When he met her in person, he thought she was so ugly that he ended the marriage as soon as he could.

Next, he fell in love with Catherine Howard. She was only sixteen. (Henry was already forty-nine.) After they were married for a little while, Henry began to think that Catherine was unfaithful to him. She, too, was sent to the Tower and beheaded.

Catherine Howard

The night before Catherine Howard died, she asked for the block she would be executed on to be brought to her room in the Tower. She wanted to practice putting her neck on it.

Only Henry's last wife, Catherine Parr, managed to survive him.

Catherine Parr

Ghosts

Many people have reported seeing ghosts in the Tower. That's not surprising, given how many grisly deaths there have been.

The ghost seen most often is Anne Boleyn. She glides through the Tower with her head tucked under her arm.

Visitors also claim to have encountered the ghosts of the two little princes who were killed in the Tower. They are often heard playing in the garden.

A countess who was supposed to be beheaded in 1541 escaped and tried to run away. Some people say they have seen her ghost, still running.

The most unusual of all is a ghostly bear that once attacked one of the guards. It is believed to be "Old Martin," a grizzly bear that was a gift from Canada.

CHAPTER 11
Tudor Prisoners

One of Henry VIII's last victims was the Earl of Surrey. Surrey's enemies convinced Henry that Surrey was plotting against him. This was easy to do because all the courtiers were usually plotting, and Henry was always suspicious.

While Surrey was locked in the Tower, he tried to escape by climbing down the chute of the garderobe. Unfortunately, the guard noticed his empty bed. After Surrey emerged, dirty and stinking, from the privy, he was recaptured. A few days later he was executed.

When Henry VIII died, his nine-year-old son
followed him as King Edward VI. Young Edward
died a few years later. In the days after Edward's
death, there was a lot of confusion about who
should rule next. Henry VIII's oldest child was

Mary from his first marriage. She was the obvious choice. But King Henry had said that his marriage to Mary's mother had broken a religious law. This meant Mary couldn't be queen. His other daughter was Elizabeth, the daughter of Anne Boleyn who was beheaded. Since

Princess Mary

Henry had said that Anne was unfaithful, people thought Elizabeth shouldn't become queen, either.

Edward VI was a strong believer in the new Protestant religion that was introduced to England by his father. He didn't want Mary to be queen because she was a Catholic. Right before he died, he said that the person who should follow him was Lady Jane Grey. She was a cousin, and her family was not Catholic.

So Jane became queen—but only for nine days. The advisors who had been ruling for Edward, because he was a child, were in favor of Jane Grey becoming queen, at least at first. But then they turned against her. Jane was accused of treason and thrown into the Tower. She protested that she had never wanted to be queen. It was forced on her. But it was no use. A few months later, she became the third queen to be beheaded in the Tower. She was not yet seventeen.

Lady Jane Grey

So Mary became queen and quickly made the country Catholic again. Mary was afraid of her half-sister, Elizabeth. Elizabeth believed in the new religion, and she also had a good claim to the throne. So Mary had Elizabeth sent to the Tower.

People held in the Tower often entered by boat through a gate to the river Thames called the Traitors' Gate. Elizabeth was angry that she was

taken through this gate. She said she was not a traitor. She sat outside in the rain for a long time before she would to go into the Tower.

Mary had Elizabeth watched very closely. She was only allowed to walk along the roof between two towers, not in the garden. Her meals all had to be examined by the Tower staff before she could eat them. Mary wanted to be sure no one could send Elizabeth a secret message.

After a few months, Elizabeth was sent from the Tower to another castle. The next time she entered the Tower, it was to prepare to be crowned queen of England. After Mary's death in 1558, she became Queen Elizabeth I, one of England's greatest rulers.

Beefeaters

There are special guards for the Tower of London, called the Yeomen Warders. The costume they wear dates back to the Tudor period. The Yeomen Warders' nickname is "Beefeaters." No one knows exactly why.

They are responsible for performing the Ceremony of Keys. The Tower is locked and the keys safely put away, at exactly 9:53 at night. The ceremony is still performed today in the same way it has been since the fourteenth century. After the Tower is locked, the Warder meets a sentry, and they say:

Sentry: "Halt! Who comes there?"

Chief Warder: "The keys."

Sentry: "Whose keys?"

Chief Warder: "[Current ruler]'s keys."

Sentry: "Pass [Current ruler]'s keys. All is well."

The guards have never missed a night. During World War II, the ceremony was delayed because German bombs were falling. After the bombing stopped, the Warder dusted himself off and finished the ceremony.

CHAPTER 12
Great Escapes

The Tower was well guarded, with strong, high stone walls and a moat. It looked like it would be impossible to escape from. But people did.

John Gerard and John Arden were locked in the Tower in 1597. They were waiting to be executed for plotting to make England a Catholic country again.

Gerard wrote a letter to a friend outside. Part of it was written in orange juice, so that the writing became invisible once it dried. His friend knew he could make the ink appear by heating the paper.

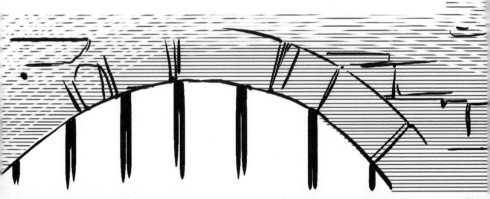

Gerard asked his guard to smuggle the letter out for him. The guard looked at the letter and saw that it didn't say anything wrong, so he agreed. The guard couldn't see the invisible orange juice writing.

Gerard and Arden managed to loosen a bolt on a door leading to the roof. They climbed to the roof of the Tower. Their friends were waiting in a boat on the river. The prisoners had brought a rope that they stretched down from the Tower roof, over the wall, and to the river. Gerard and Arden had to climb down the rope. This was especially hard for Gerard, because he had been tortured, and his hands were injured. Even so, they both made it down and escaped. Gerard survived for another forty years, and lived to be seventy-three.

An especially risky escape plan was carried out by the wife of the Earl of Nithsdale. Nithsdale had been condemned to death for his part in an uprising against King George I in 1715. His wife

arranged to visit him in the Tower with a group of women. One very slender woman secretly wore an extra set of clothing.

In the Tower, they dressed Lord Nithsdale in the

Lord Nithsdale and his wife

extra women's clothing. They put makeup and a wig on him. There wasn't time to shave his beard off, so they painted it white. When the group of ladies left, Nithsdale was in the middle of their group. He walked with his head bowed as though he were crying, so no one could see his face.

Lady Nithsdale stayed behind in the cell. She carried on a fake conversation as though her husband were still there. When she thought enough time had passed, she left the cell. She asked the guards not to disturb her husband because he was praying. Lord Nithsdale was never captured, and spent the rest of his life in France.

Torture

The Tower of London was not designed to be a dungeon. Most of the prisoners in the Tower of London were not tortured. However, the Tudor rulers did use torture when they wanted to force someone to confess. The most common method was the rack. This was used on both men and women. A person was stretched out with their hands and feet tied to the corners of the rack. Then the rack was tightened so their body was pulled more and more. Eventually this would tear their limbs out of their sockets.

The other common method was manacles. People were hung up by their wrists so their feet didn't touch the ground. This was extremely painful, and after a while it could do permanent harm to the hands and arms.

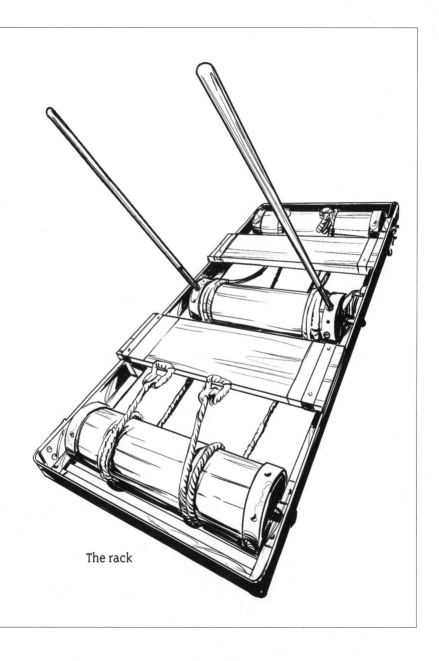

The rack

CHAPTER 13
The Tower Today

After Elizabeth I became queen, the Tower was used less and less as a palace. It was still an important military site and a prison for political prisoners until the mid-1800s.

Executions on Tower Hill continued to be a popular public event. In 1747, Lord Lovat was to be executed for plotting against the king. Stands were put up to seat all the people who wanted to watch. But so many people crowded onto the stands that one of them broke, killing twenty people. Lovat thought this was very funny. He died laughing. Lovat was the very last person to be executed on Tower Hill.

The Tower became important again for military reasons during World War I. It was used to store gunpowder and supplies. It also served as a center for recruiting soldiers. And once again it was a place of execution. During the war, eleven foreign spies were put to death there. However, they were not beheaded or hanged. They were shot by a firing squad.

During World War II, Victory Gardens were planted at the Tower. The moat had been filled in, and people used the land to grow vegetables

to help feed the country. During the war, parts of the Tower were destroyed by German bombs. One bomb just missed the White Tower.

Josef Jakobs

For a while Rudolf Hess, Hitler's right-hand man, was held prisoner in the Tower. And the very last person ever to be executed there was Josef Jakobs, a German spy who was shot in 1941.

The Tower was no longer a fort or a palace. Another role was becoming the most important. As early as the seventeenth century, the Tower was a popular tourist site. So many people were coming to see the Menagerie that an admission fee began to be charged. (But for a while you could get in for free if you brought a dog or cat to feed to the lions!) By the nineteenth century, a ticket office had to be set up to control the crowds.

Today the Tower is one of the most popular tourist attractions in all of England. It attracts more than two million visitors a year. People come to see the Crown Jewels, and the graffiti scratched on the walls by prisoners. Standing on Tower Green, people can see the very spot where three English queens were beheaded. And in the White Tower, they can touch walls that have seen almost every important event in England for over a thousand years.

Timeline of the Tower of London

AD 43 — Romans build a fort on the site of present-day London

1066 — The first fortress is built on the site of the Tower of London

1078 — Construction begins on the stone tower that will become the White Tower

1255 — First elephant in England arrives at the Tower

1322 — Ceremony of the Keys, which is still performed today, begins

1381 — The Tower is invaded during the Peasants' Revolt

1483 — The two "Little Princes in the Tower" disappear, probably murdered

1485 — Yeoman Warders officially established

1536 — Queen Anne Boleyn beheaded in the Tower

1618 — Sir Walter Raleigh taken from the Tower to be beheaded

1660 — Sightseers are admitted to the Tower for the first time

1671 — Colonel Blood attempts to steal the Crown Jewels

1674 — Skeletons of two children believed to be the two little princes are dug up

1747 — Lord Lovat becomes the last person executed on Tower Hill

1831–35 — Menagerie is moved from the Tower to the London Zoo

1941 — Josef Jakobs, a German spy, is the last person to be executed in the Tower

1994 — The Jewel House at the Tower opens to display the Crown Jewels

Timeline of the World

AD 49	Paul's Epistle to the Galatians, part of the New Testament, is written
1066	William the Conqueror invades England
1206	Genghis Khan becomes Great Khan of the Mongol Empire
1215	Magna Carta, giving some Englishmen basic rights, is signed
1337	Beginning of the Hundred Years' War
1348	The Black Death kills almost half the population of London
1420	Construction on the Chinese Forbidden City is completed
1492	Christopher Columbus sails to the New World
1531	Church of England breaks away from the Catholic Church
1543	Copernicus publishes his theory that the sun is the center of the solar system
1559	Queen Elizabeth I is crowned
1649	Puritans execute King Charles I
1660	King Charles II restored to the English throne
1666	Great Fire of London
1776	America adopts the Declaration of Independence
1837	Queen Victoria is crowned
1939	World War II begins
1953	Queen Elizabeth II is crowned
1994	The Channel Tunnel opens, connecting England and France

Bibliography

*Books for young readers

Borman, Tracy. *The Story of the Tower of London*. London:
Merrell Publishers, 2015.

*Fisher, Leonard Everett. *The Tower of London*. New York:
Macmillan, 1987.

Jones, Nigel. *Tower: An Epic History of the Tower of London*.
New York: St. Martin's Press, 2011.

Websites

Tower of London: Historic Royal Palaces.
www.hrp.org.uk/tower-of-london/#gs.HYGsTAY

Tower of London—UNESCO World Heritage Centre.
whc.unesco.org/en/list/488